INCREDIBLE INFOGRAPHICS!

CONTENTS

Written by Jilly Hunt

Illustrated by Mark Ruffle

Collins

1 INFOGRAPHICS

Infographics are pictures or diagrams that show information. This book is stuffed full of infographics about the world. There are lots of facts to explore about different features of planet Earth. You can find out about the world's tallest mountains or how deep the ocean is.

Sometimes you might not know where to start looking at an infographic. Here are a few tips:

1
Look at the heading. This will give you your first clue about the information you'll see.

2
Look at the picture. What does it show?

3
Read the labels to find out more.

4
Think about what you've seen and read. How does it fit together?

BIG NUMBERS

You're about to read some big facts. Some of these big facts come with big numbers. Here's a reminder about how we say big numbers:

1 = one

10 = ten

100 = one hundred

1,000 = one thousand

10,000 = ten thousand

100,000 = one hundred thousand

1,000,000 = one million

10,000,000 = ten million

100,000,000 = one hundred million

1,000,000,000 = one billion

2 PLANET EARTH

The world is a massive **sphere**. It measures approximately 40,000 kilometres around its **circumference**.

WHICH IS THE BIGGEST CONTINENT?

1. ASIA

Land area: 44,579,000 km²
Population: 4,694,576,167
Biggest country: Russia

2. AFRICA

Land area: 30,244,000 km²
Population: 1,393,676,444
Biggest country: Algeria

3. NORTH AMERICA

Land area: 24,239,000 km²
Population: 595,000,000
Biggest country: Canada

4. SOUTH AMERICA

Land area: 17,814,000 km²
Population: 434,254,119
Biggest country: Brazil

A space shuttle takes 90 minutes to go all the way round the world. It can travel at an incredibly fast speed of around 27,880 kilometres per hour.

It could take a human over 8,300 hours to walk all the way around the world. That's almost a whole year!

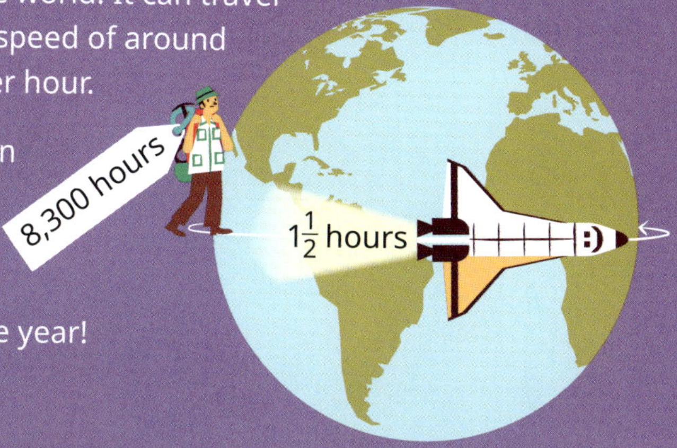

5. ANTARCTICA

Land area: 14,200,000 km^2
Population: 1,000–5,000
Biggest country: There are no countries

6. EUROPE

Land area: 10,180,000 km^2
Population: 745,173,774
Biggest country: Russia

7. OCEANIA

Land area: 8,511,000 km^2
Population: 44,491,724
Biggest country: Australia

Which **continent** do you live on?

COUNTRIES OF THE WORLD

Can you guess what the biggest country in the world is?

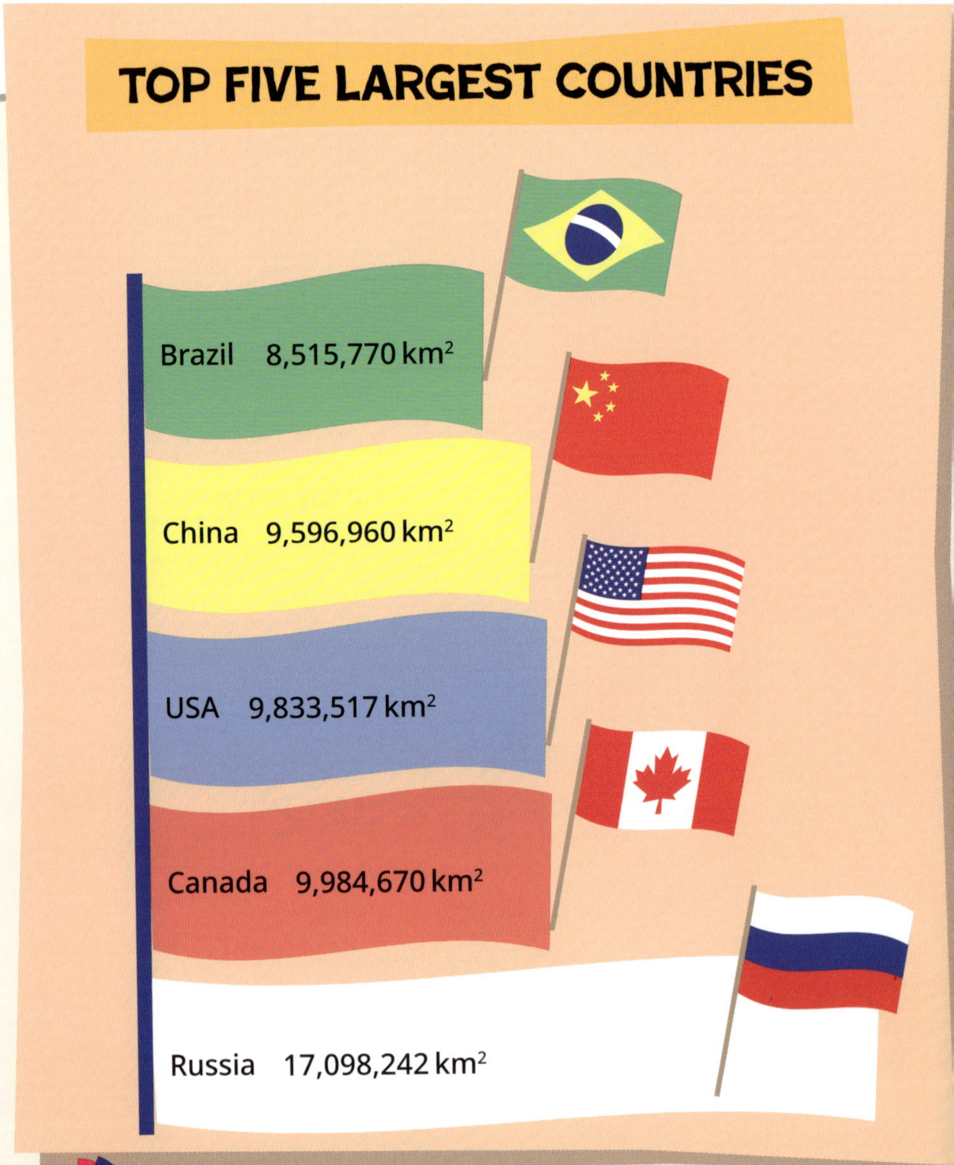

Billions of football pitches would fit into a space the size of Russia. Only 63 football pitches would fit into the space of the world's smallest country. It's so small you could walk around it in less than an hour.

TOP FIVE SMALLEST COUNTRIES

BIOMES OF THE WORLD

Around the world, there are regions that have a similar **climate** and **landscape**. The same kinds of plants and animals live in these areas. These regions are called biomes.

SIX MAIN TYPES OF BIOMES

RAINFORESTS

Rainforests have wet and dry seasons, but the temperature stays about the same all year. This creates good growing conditions for trees and other plants. One tree in the Amazon rainforest has grown 88.5 metres tall! That's as tall as a 25-storey tower block.

GRASSLANDS

Not surprisingly, grasses are the main plants on grasslands. There are different types of grassland around the world. Most have hot summers and cold winters.

DESERTS

Deserts are regions that have very little rainfall. Deserts can be hot or cold. In hot deserts, like the Sahara, animals often only come out at night when it's cooler. The Gobi Desert in Central Asia is one of the coldest deserts. Its name means "waterless place" in Mongolian.

TUNDRA

Tundra regions have long, cold winters and short summers. The name "tundra" comes from the Finnish word "tunturi" which means treeless plain.

Around the North Pole is the Arctic tundra. This area is known for being cold and covered in snow. Despite this, over 400 types of flowers grow here in the summer.

SAVANNAH

Savannah regions are warm or hot. They are covered with grass and have some trees. Savannah has a dry season and a wet season. When the rains come, the plants grow quickly. Some grasses can grow over two centimetres in just one day!

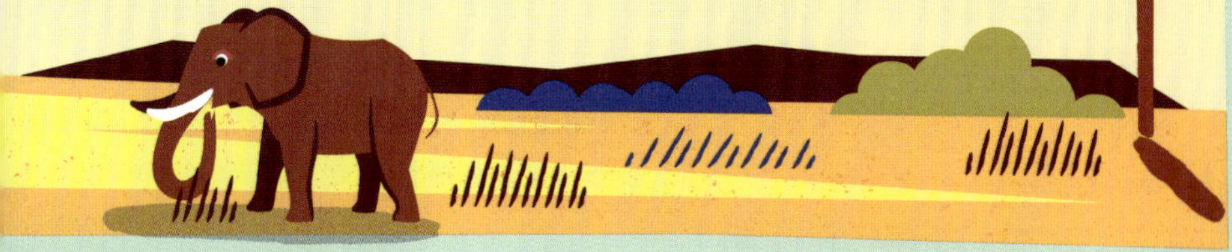

WOODLANDS

Trees are the main plants found in woodlands. Different types of trees grow in woodlands, depending on the climate.

A WORLD OF EXTREMES

Planet Earth has some surprising extremes. Can you guess where the driest place or the hottest place on Earth might be?

HOTTEST, DRIEST, COLDEST, WETTEST

The hottest place on Earth is part of the Mojave Desert, USA. In 1913, Furnace Creek, Death Valley, reached a record-breaking temperature of 56.7 degrees Celsius.

One of the driest places in the world is the Atacama Desert, Chile. Some parts of the desert have less than two millimetres of rain per year. Have a look on a ruler to see how little one millimetre is.

The wettest place on Earth is a village in India called Mawsynram. About 11,971 millimetres of rain falls every year – that's deeper than most swimming pools!

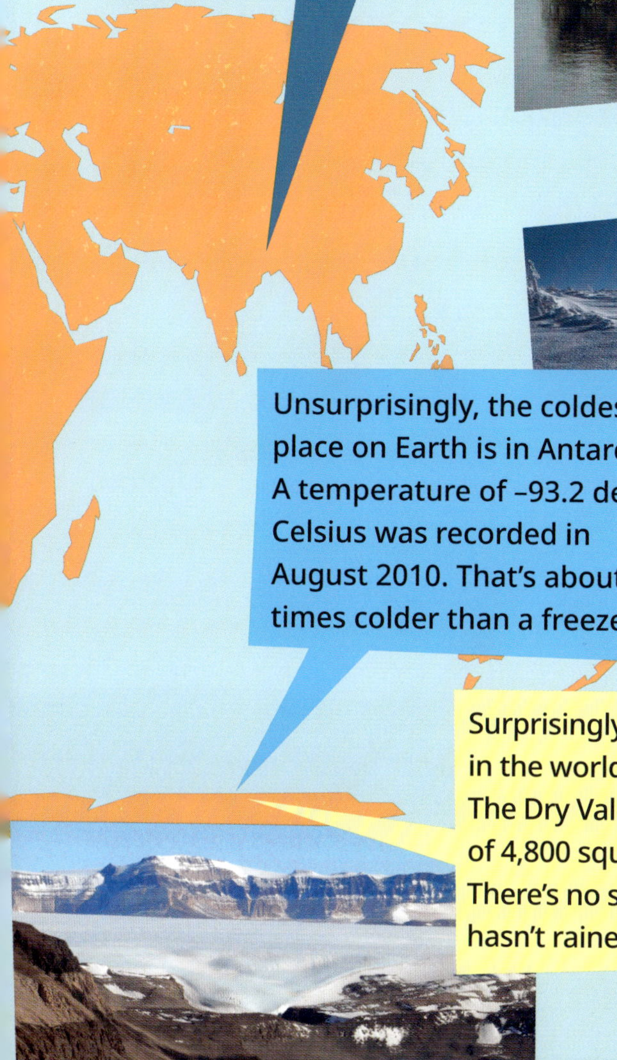

Unsurprisingly, the coldest place on Earth is in Antarctica. A temperature of –93.2 degrees Celsius was recorded in August 2010. That's about five times colder than a freezer!

Surprisingly, the driest region in the world is in Antarctica. The Dry Valleys cover an area of 4,800 square kilometres. There's no snow or ice here and it hasn't rained for millions of years!

3 FROM PEAKS TO EXPLOSIONS

Have you ever wondered how mountains form? Let's take a look at how some of the world's tallest mountains were formed.

MAKING TALL MOUNTAINS

1. Deep underneath the ground is the Earth's crust. This crust is made up of enormous rocky sections called tectonic plates. All of the world's land and water sit on these solid plates.

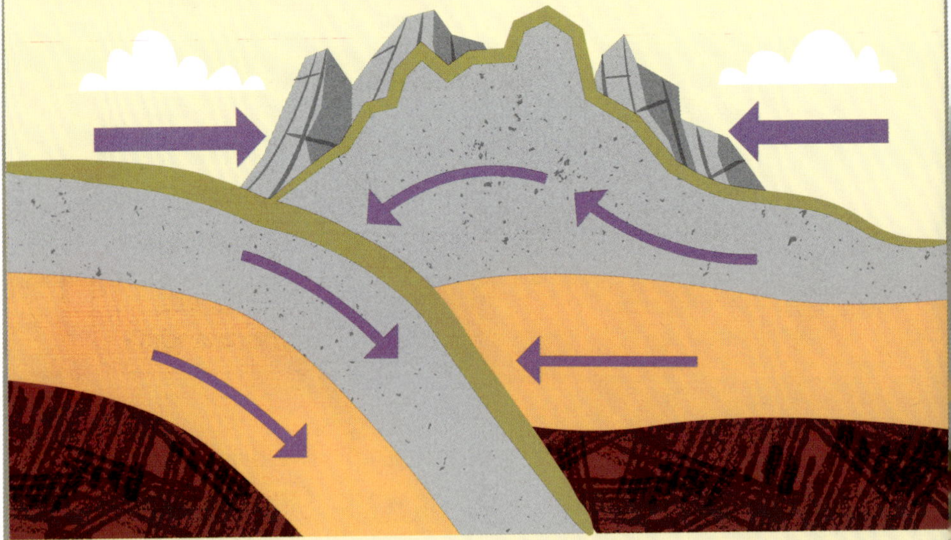

2. Tectonic plates are slowly moving. Where one plate meets another plate, they push against each other. One plate is forced up and folds to form hills or mountains. These mountains are called "fold mountains".

THE WORLD'S TALLEST FOLD MOUNTAINS

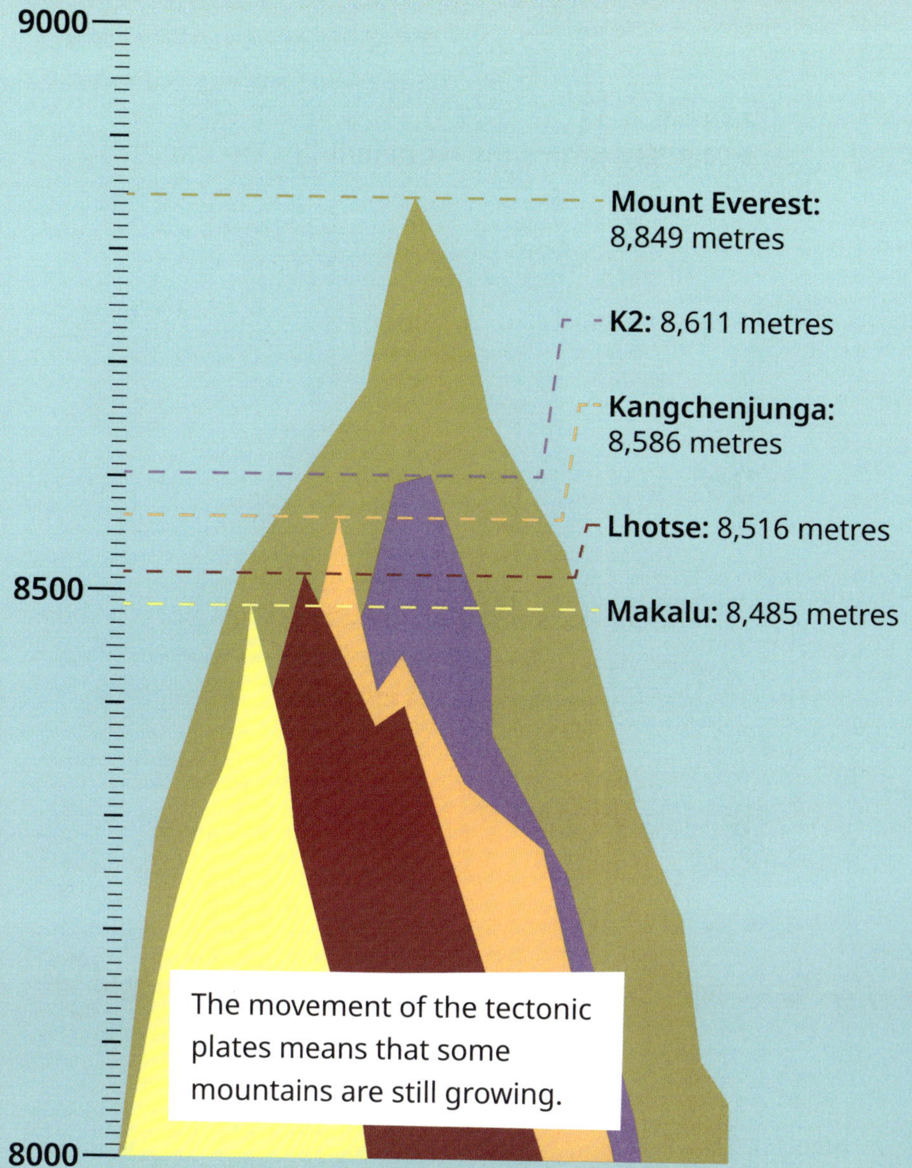

The movement of the tectonic plates means that some mountains are still growing.

VOLCANOES

Volcanoes are another type of mountain. Volcanoes can form when tectonic plates move apart in opposite directions. This leaves a gap in Earth's crust, out of which **lava** erupts. This lava builds up to form a mountain.

MAGMA AND LAVA

Magma is **molten** lava. It's extremely hot, reaching temperatures between 700 degrees Celsius and 1,300 degrees Celsius. When magma reaches the surface, it is called lava.

Lava can reach speeds of about 60 kilometres per hour!

There's a volcano on the island of Java that spews out blue lava.

THE POWER OF VOLCANOES

The power of a volcanic eruption is measured on its own scale. It's called the Volcanic Explosivity Index, or VEI for short. The scale goes from zero to eight. It is a measure of how much magma is thrown out.

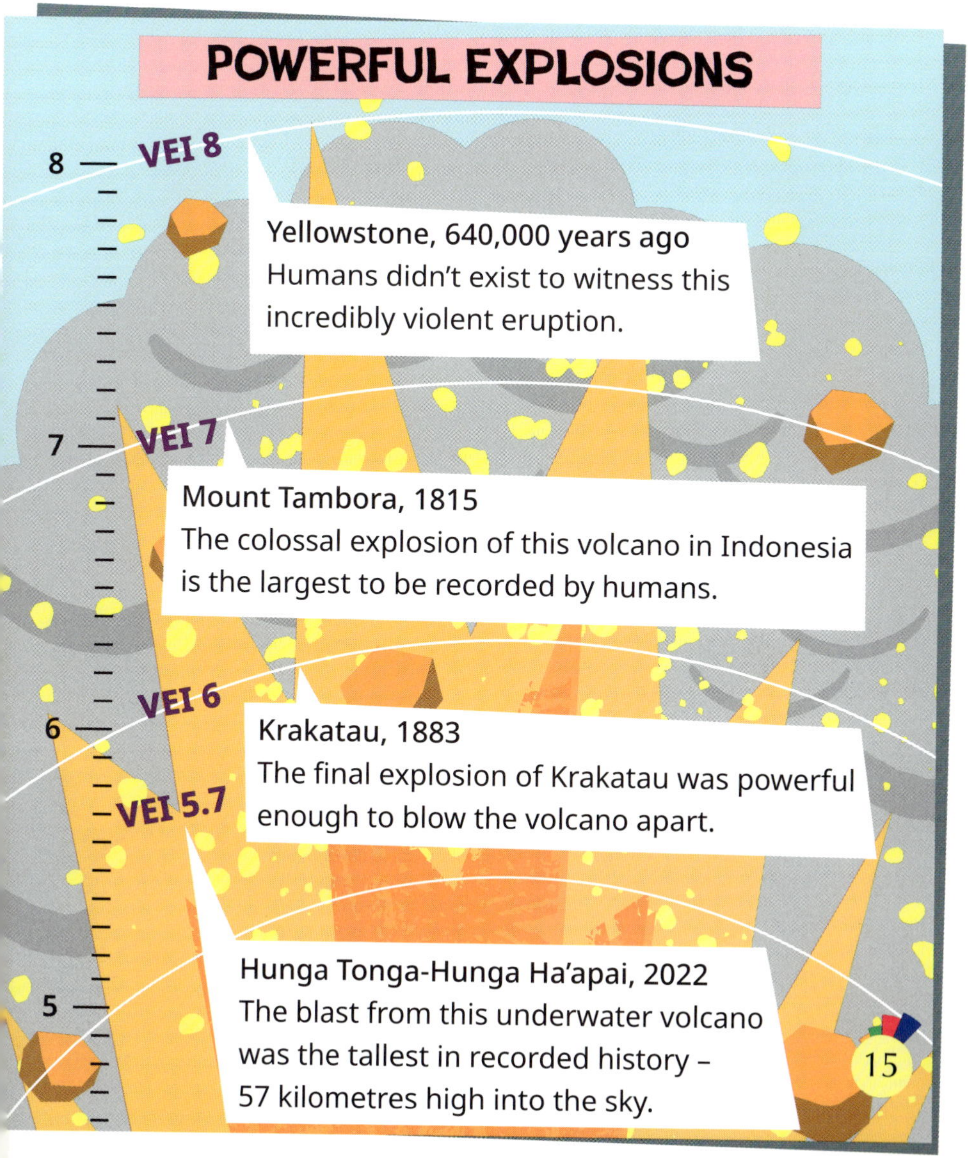

EARTHQUAKES

An earthquake is when the ground shakes. Earthquakes are caused by the movement of Earth's tectonic plates. Most earthquakes happen in the area where tectonic plates meet each other, which is called the plate boundary. Energy is built up as the plates move. Eventually, this energy is released and causes Earth to shake.

Earthquakes are measured on their own scale that goes from one to ten. We call it the Earthquake Magnitude Scale. Some earthquakes are small and are hardly felt, but others are so powerful that they destroy whole towns and cities.

THE FIVE BIGGEST EARTHQUAKES

9.5 — Valdivia, Chile, 1960

9.2 — Alaska, USA, 1964

9.1 — Tohoku, Japan, 2011

9.1 — Sumatra, Indonesia, 2004

9.0 — Severo-Kurilsk, Russia, 1952

In Japanese mythology, a giant catfish was believed to be the cause of earthquakes.

4 A WORLD OF WATER

Most of Earth's surface is covered in water. Where does all this water come from?

All the water in the world follows the water cycle. As it moves, it may change state. This means it can go from liquid water to solid ice, or into a gas called water vapour.

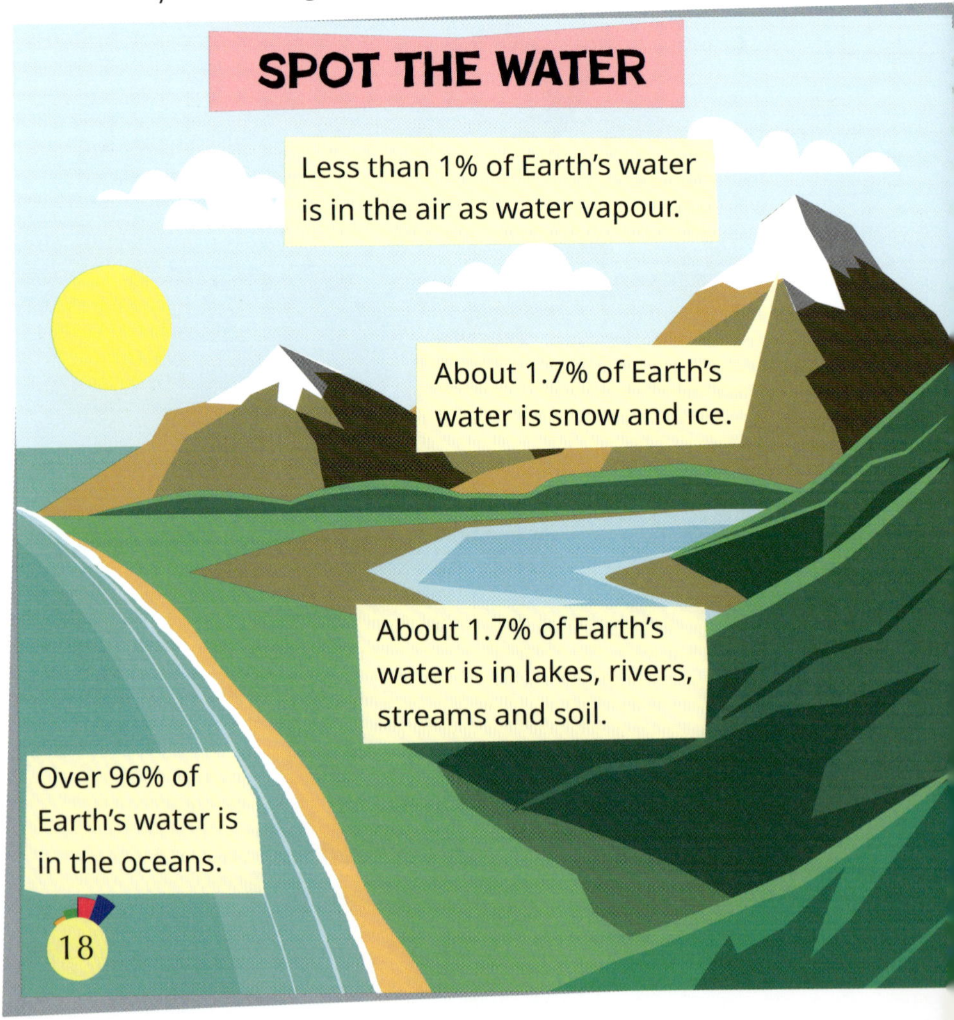

THE WATER CYCLE

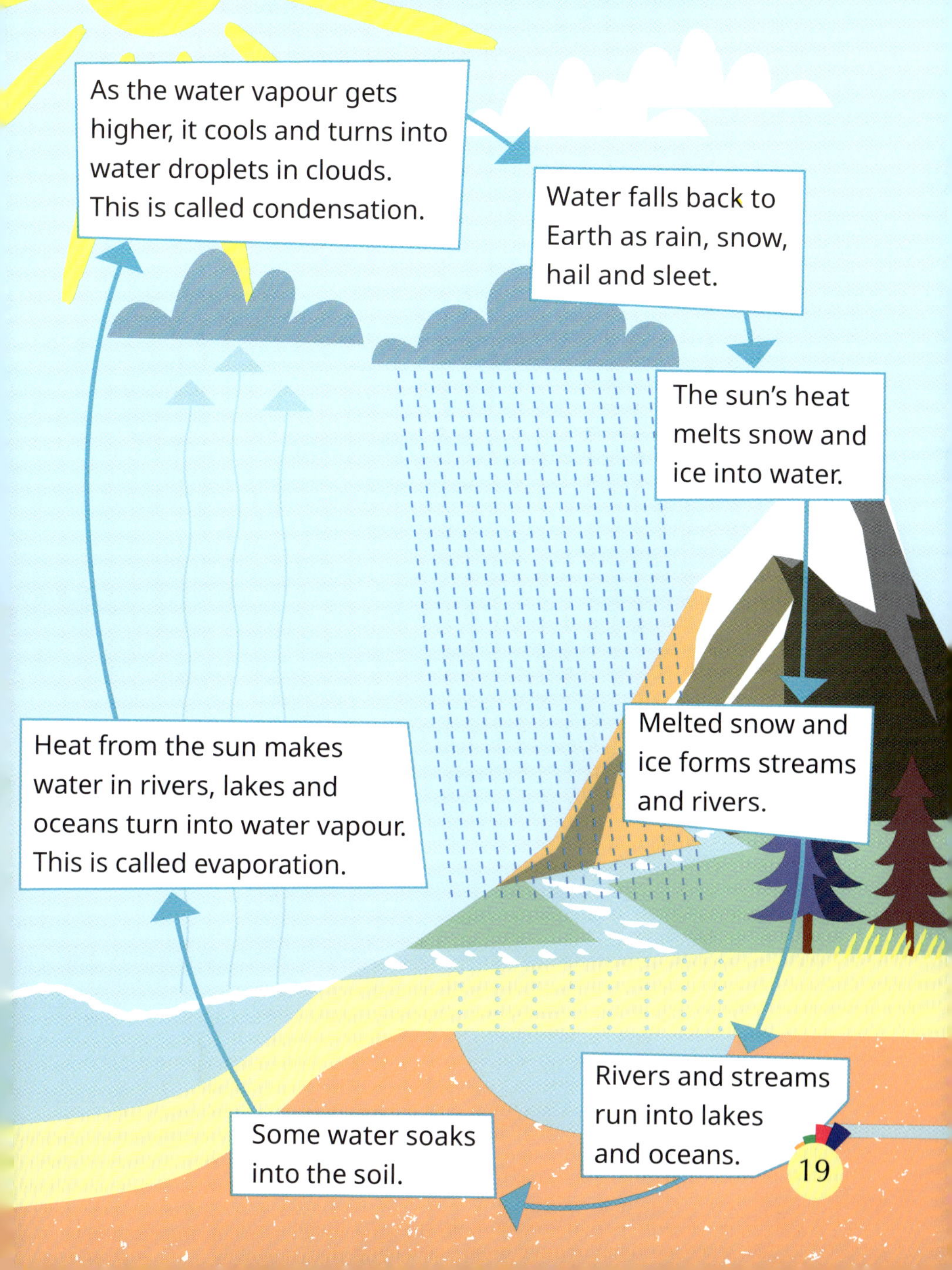

RIVERS

How long are the world's rivers? It's often tricky to know exactly because rivers can change course over time. The start, or source, of a river can be hard to find. It's sometimes just a small trickle of water up high in a mountain.

THE LONGEST RIVERS

YENISEY RIVER – 5,539 KILOMETRES

The Yenisey River starts in Mongolia and runs through Russia, ending at the Arctic Ocean.

MISSISSIPPI RIVER – 5,971 KILOMETRES

The Mississippi is the longest river in North America.

CHANG JIANG RIVER – 6,300 KILOMETRES

The Chang Jiang River is the longest river in just one country.

AMAZON RIVER – 6,400 KILOMETRES

The Amazon River is the largest river in the world by the amount of water it carries.

NILE RIVER – 6,650 KILOMETRES

The Nile carries the smallest amount of water of all of the world's major rivers.

OCEANS

The world's oceans are so big that people are still learning about them.

OCEAN DEPTHS

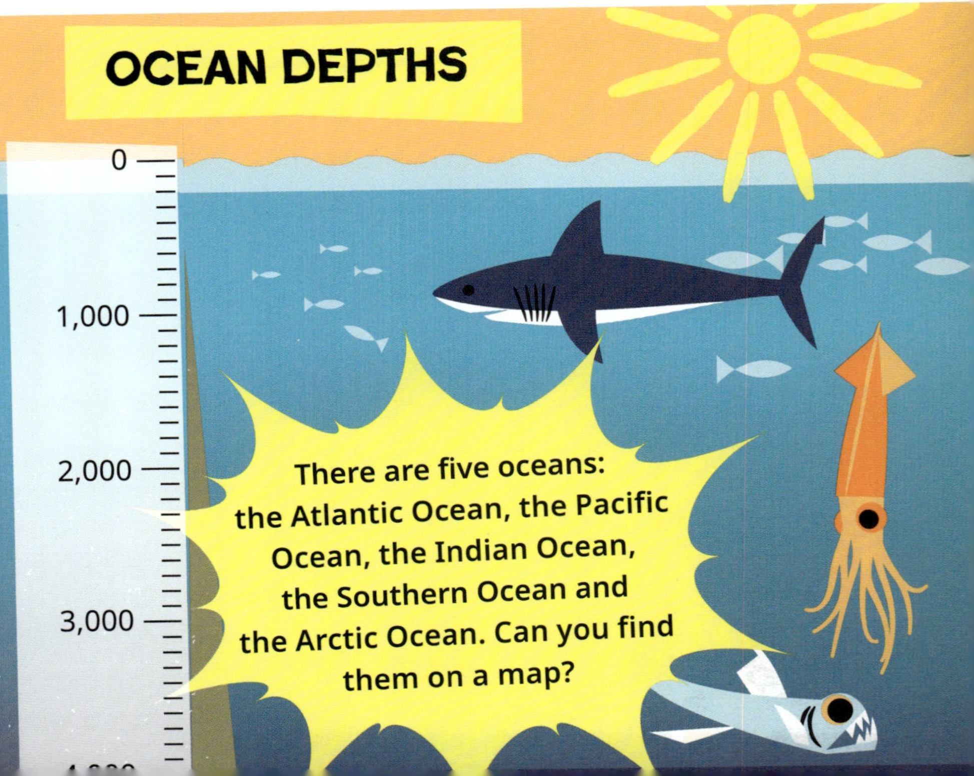

THE SUNLIGHT ZONE

This zone is the lightest and the water is warmed by the sun.

THE TWILIGHT ZONE

Sunlight is very faint in this zone. The fish that live in this zone often have big eyes to help them see better.

There are five oceans: the Atlantic Ocean, the Pacific Ocean, the Indian Ocean, the Southern Ocean and the Arctic Ocean. Can you find them on a map?

THE MIDNIGHT ZONE

The only light in this zone comes from animals that can make it themselves.

THE ABYSS

It is pitch-black and the water is almost freezing cold.

THE TRENCHES

Very little lives this deep.

CHALLENGER DEEP

This is the deepest point of the ocean.

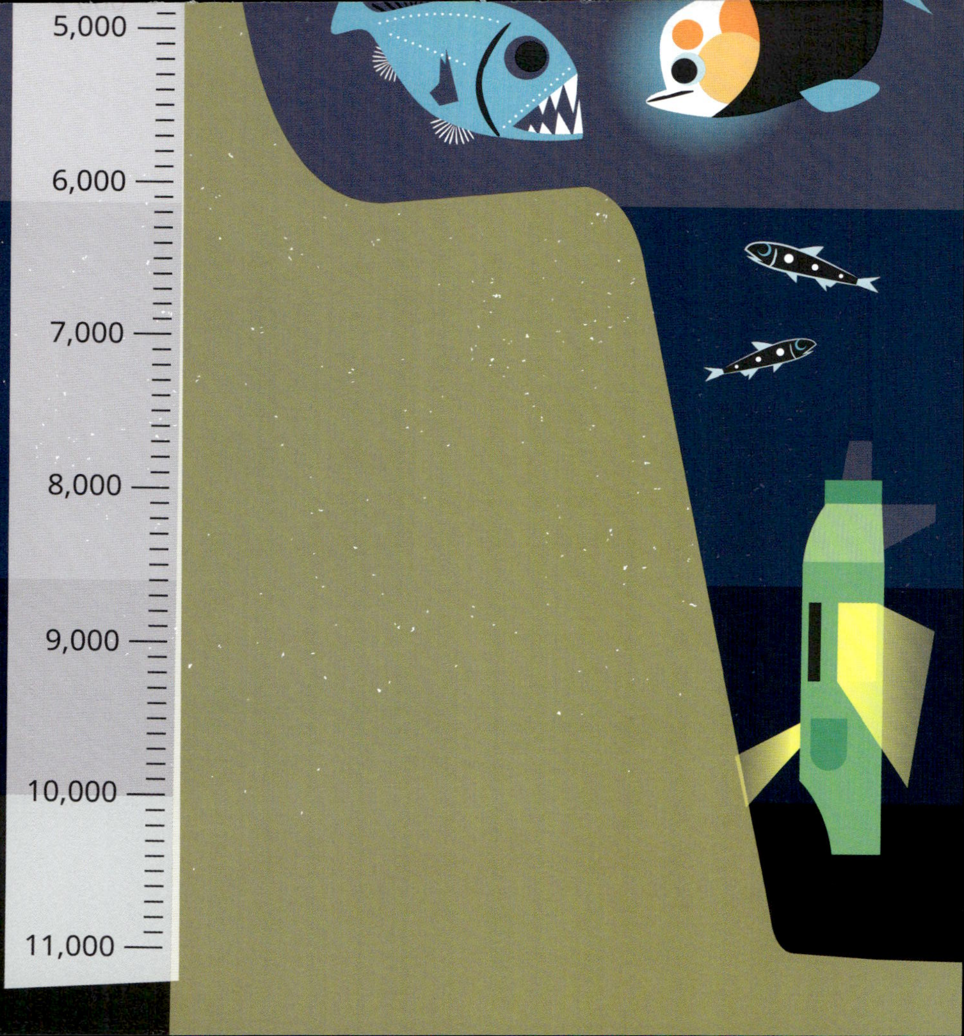

5 PEOPLE IN THE WORLD

How many people live in the world? This number is continually changing as people are born and people die. In November 2022, the world population reached eight billion for the first time. It's expected to grow by nearly two billion by 2050.

Eight billion is a lot of people. Where do they all live?

COUNTRIES WITH THE HIGHEST POPULATION

CHINA – 1,416,043,270

INDIA – 1,409,128,296

UNITED STATES – 336,673,595

INDONESIA – 281,562,465

PAKISTAN – 252,363,571

You might not be surprised to find out that the world's smallest countries also have some of the smallest populations.

POPULATION OF THE SMALLEST COUNTRIES

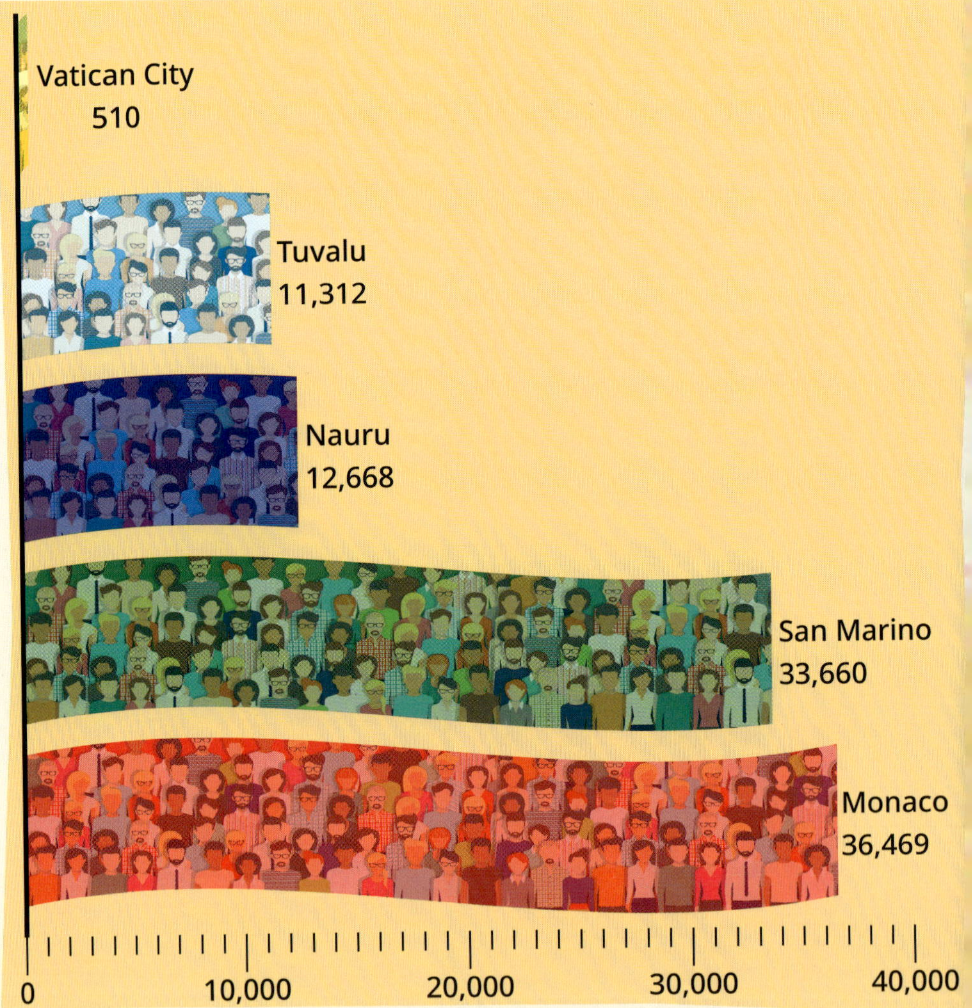

Some cities have more people living in them than in some countries.

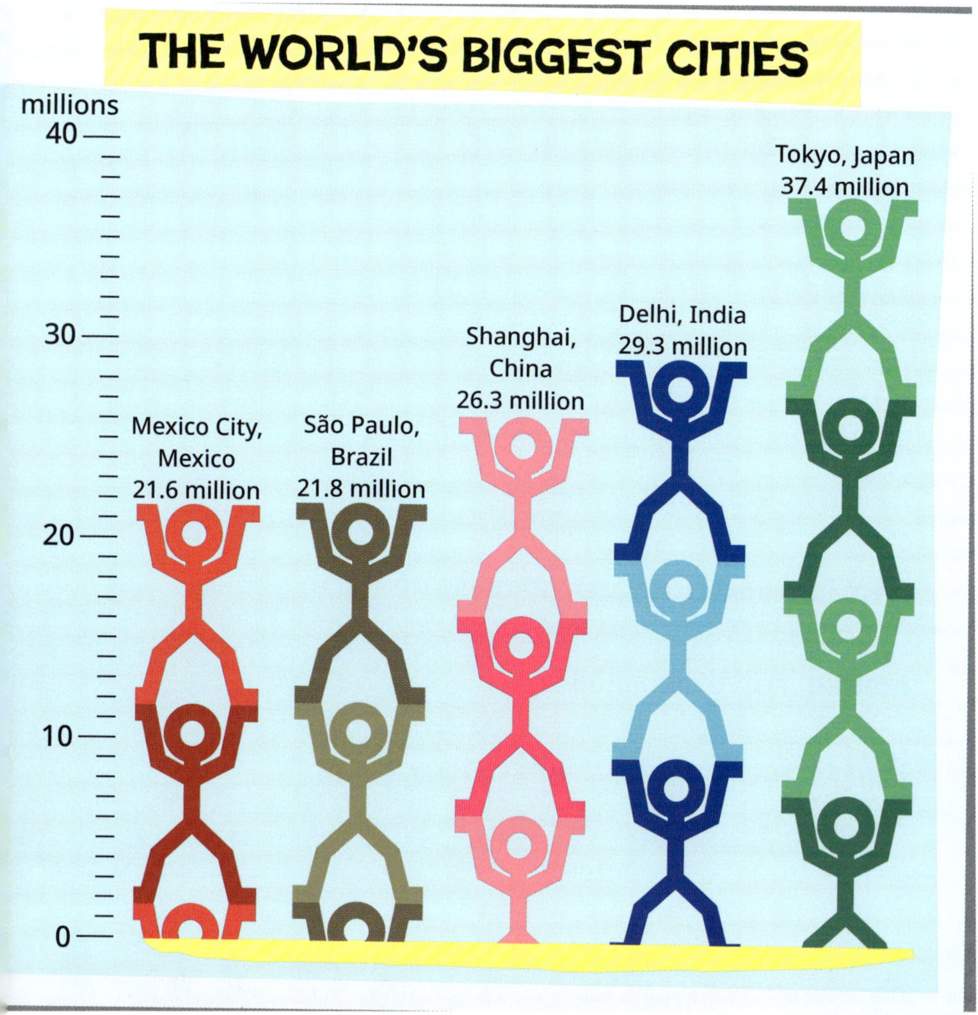

Infographics can help us to visualise huge numbers, and understand the world we live in better. Can you think of other ways of representing the world around you?

GLOSSARY

circumference the distance around the edge of a round object

climate the average weather and temperature of a place

continent a large, solid area of land, consisting of different countries

landscape what you can see in an area of land, for example, rivers, mountains, fields

lava hot liquid rock from underneath Earth's crust

molten hot, thick liquid

sphere round in shape, for example, a ball

INDEX

BIGGEST, LONGEST, HIGHEST, DEEPEST

Can you remember which is the biggest, longest, highest, deepest?

Ideas for reading

Written by Gill Matthews
Primary Literacy Consultant

Reading objectives:

- check that the text makes sense to them, discuss their understanding and explaining the meaning of words in context
- identify main ideas drawn from more than one paragraph and summarising these
- identify how language, structure, and presentation contribute to meaning
- retrieve and record information from non-fiction

Spoken language objectives:

- articulate and justify answers, arguments and opinions
- use spoken language to develop understanding through speculating, hypothesising, imagining and exploring ideas
- participate in discussions, presentations, performances, role play, improvisations and debates

Curriculum links: Geography: locational knowledge

Interest words: hottest, driest, wettest, biggest, largest, smallest, coldest, tallest

Resources: World map or globe

Build a context for reading

- Ask children to look at the front cover of the book and to read the title. Discuss what they think the book might be about. Encourage them to support their responses with reasons and evidence.
- Read the back-cover blurb. Ask children what they think they are going to find out from reading the book. Are they able to suggest answers to the questions in the blurb?
- Point out that this is an information book. Ask what kind of features the children expect it to have.
- Ask children to find the contents page. Discuss the purpose and organisation of a contents page.